We need to regain *validit*
the sight of the world. The p
both poor and pathetic. M
with reality and irrelevant to
credibility. The church has
need renewing by the Spiri

What difference will it make?

Jesus said that his Spirit would be 'another Helper' (John 14:16) who would be to us what Jesus was to his disciples.

The Holy Spirit comes, said Jesus, to give us a new birth and a new life (John 3:3-8). He assures us of our relationship with God (Romans 8:15-17). He helps us to pray and to open our hearts in worship (Romans 8:26; John 4:24). He empowers us in our witness to Christ (Acts 1:8). He equips us with spiritual gifts (1 Corinthians 12:1-11). He enables us to understand God's word (Ephesians 1:17-18; 1 Corinthians 2:6-16). He strengthens us to overcome temptation (Romans 8:2). He continually wants to pour God's love into our hearts (Romans 5:5). He makes us steadily more like Jesus (2 Corinthians 3:17-18; Galatians 5:16-25).

In all these areas (and others too) we *have* to depend on the Holy Spirit. We cannot do it ourselves. Much of the church's life lacks the reality of God's presence because it rests on human wisdom and effort. Only the Spirit gives life (2 Corinthians 3:6).

When, however, God wants to do something new in our lives, there is nearly always a spiritual battle: 'For what our human nature wants is opposed to what the Spirit wants' (Galatians 5:17). The devil also is out to confuse and destroy God's work. We have clear warnings about this in the Scriptures.

Three exhortations

1. Don't resist the Holy Spirit

In Acts 7 Stephen spoke boldly to the religious leaders of his day: 'How deaf you are to God's message! You are just like your ancestors: you too have always resisted the Holy Spirit!' (verse 51).

God is always doing something new among his people. The Spirit of God is the Spirit of movement. He is always seeking to make the church fresh and relevant for every age and culture. However, with each new work of the Spirit there will always be excesses and abuses. The great mistake is so to concentrate on these that we fail to appreciate, and respond to, the new life that the Spirit is genuinely bringing into our lives. The answer to *mis*-use is not *dis*-use, but *right* use. If we cling firmly to the particular patterns and traditions that we already know, we may find ourselves resisting the Spirit. We must always be open to the new thing that God is doing among us.

2. Don't quench the Holy Spirit

So Paul wrote to the Thessalonian church. It seems that some of the leaders and older members were disapproving of certain spiritual gifts, especially prophecy. It may have been that these gifts were mostly expressed by the younger Christians, so Paul exhorted them 'to pay proper respect to those who work among you'. However, Paul also told the leaders: 'Do not restrain [or quench] the Holy Spirit; do not despise inspired messages. Put all things to the test: keep what is good and avoid every kind of evil' (1 Thessalonians 5:12-22).

Tensions and splits in churches usually come when some Christians push certain aspects of the Spirit's work too hard and the leaders oppose them too strongly. Both parties are thus guilty of quenching the fire of the Spirit in that church.

3. Don't grieve the Holy Spirit

Paul warned the Ephesian Christians that they would grieve the Spirit if, in any way, their relationships with one another were wrong. Any deceit or anger, dishonesty or criticism, bitterness or hatred, immorality or greed, would 'make God's Holy Spirit sad'. Instead, he said, 'be kind and tender-hearted to one another, and forgive one another, as God has forgiven you through Christ' (Ephesians 4:25 – 5:21).

In the history of the church, almost every spiritual renewal has been preceded by Christians sorting out their relationships with each other: forgiving and asking for forgiveness, turning away from all known sin, and seeking to walk in love.

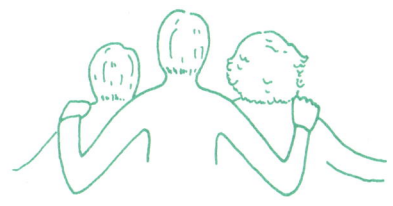

How can we be renewed?

In one sense there is nothing you or I can do. Jesus likened the Spirit to the wind, and 'the wind blows wherever it wishes; you hear the sound it makes, but you do not know where it comes from or where it is going . . .' (John 3:8). However, although no one can create or control the wind, we can each put ourselves in a place where we can experience the wind when it blows. We can throw open the windows and doors to let the fresh breeze come in, and we can also do the same with our lives by opening them to the Spirit.

The disciples once saw Jesus at prayer. They were obviously attracted by the depth of relationship between God the Son and God the Father. They too longed for a deeper experience of God, so they asked him, 'Lord, teach us to pray...'. In reply, Jesus gave them the Lord's Prayer, as we know it today. Then he went on specifically to promise them the gift of the Holy Spirit. The Spirit would help them to pray. The Spirit would deepen their experience of God. The Spirit would continually make their lives fresh and new.

'The Father in heaven [will] give the Holy Spirit to those who ask him!' said Jesus (Luke 11:13).

Hindrances

In practice, however, there are various hindrances which either prevent some people from asking in the first place, or, when they do ask, stop them from receiving. What are these hindrances?

1. Confusion

'Did you receive the Holy Spirit when you became believers?' asked the apostle Paul to some disciples at Ephesus (Acts 19:2). It is clear that they knew little or nothing about the Spirit.

In recent years there has been much debate about the work of the Holy Spirit, leaving many Christians suspicious, enthusiastic or confused. We need to learn from Paul's instructions to the Corinthian church in the New Testament. Paul acknowledged that they had been enriched with every spiritual gift, but they had got things out of proportion. They were 'high' on the more spectacular gifts, but less excited about humble, practical service. Paul wrote to correct the imbalance. He reminded them that even the least gifted Christians were indispensable members of the body of Christ. They all needed one another, since they all belonged to the one body (1 Corinthians 12).

Some Christians today need to beware of overstressing the spectacular, searching constantly for new experiences, exaggerating stories of healings and deliverances. God doubtless longs to demonstrate the power of his kingdom far more convincingly than we allow him to – but we must beware of being insensitive towards those who do not share exactly the same emphases and convictions, but who are still true Christians. God has blessed all Christians with 'every spiritual blessing', wrote Paul (Ephesians 1:3). There is no first-class or second-class membership within the church of Jesus Christ. None of us have fully experienced all the 'infinite riches of Christ'. Whatever we may have experienced, there is much more to come; but it is all there in Christ.

At the same time, it is not enough to claim that we have 'got it all' and so have nothing to seek. It is possible to have all the right words or actions, but little evidence of spiritual life. Paul prayed earnestly that the Ephesian Christians, who had 'every spiritual blessing in Christ', should still come 'to know his love — although it can never be fully known — and so be completely filled with the very nature of God' (3:19). The Corinthian Christians were also urged to let love be their first and foremost aim, but also, to 'set your hearts on spiritual gifts' (1 Corinthians 14:1).

Another hindrance to being filled with the Spirit is:

2. Lack of personal commitment

Jesus gave the promise of the Spirit to those who were already his disciples. They had already committed themselves, at least in some measure, to Jesus as their Lord and Saviour. Until Jesus is Lord of my life, I cannot know his Spirit filling my life. God gives the Spirit to those who are willing to obey him (Acts 5:32); and it is only by the power of his Spirit that we are able to obey him.

A simple illustration may help. Suppose I hold a book in my hand and place a glove over my wrist. Then I tell the glove, 'Pick up that book!' It cannot do it. Suppose, with

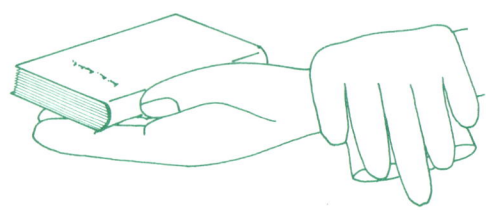

my other hand, I give the glove a perfect example by picking up the book. 'Now glove, pick up that book!' It still cannot do it. God the Father has told us what to do, but you and I cannot do it. God the Son has given us a perfect example, but still you and I cannot do it.

What the glove needs, and what you and I need, is a living power within. Then we can begin to do what God the Father has told us and what God the Son has shown us. Just as the glove needs the hand and is powerless without it, so you and I need the Holy Spirit and are powerless without him.

Further, although every true Christian has the Holy Spirit (Romans 8:9), not every true Christian is filled with the Spirit. 'Be filled with the Spirit' (Ephesians 5:18) is a command which has to be obeyed.

To continue with the glove illustration: if I put my hand partially in the glove, the glove can do some things (such as push the book around), but it cannot work as I want it to work. Only as the glove 'yields' fully to the power of my hand, and 'allows' my hand to fill every part of the glove, can it work as I want it to work.

In the same way, it is only as we yield fully to the lordship of Christ, and allow his Spirit to fill every part of our life, that we can work as God wants us to work. We must first be wholeheartedly committed to Jesus Christ as Lord. Lack of commitment will hinder us from being filled with the Spirit.

3. Complacency

Why bother? Am I not all right as I am? What's all the fuss about? Apathy, complacency — common marks of today's society — have crept into much of the church.

Jesus therefore set the promise of the Spirit in the context of the parable of 'the friend at midnight'. A man has a late-night visitor, but realizes he has no food in his house to offer him — a vivid picture of many Christians who feel unable to help those who are spiritually hungry and needy all around them. However, because the man in the story is genuinely concerned for the needs of his friend, he is willing to disturb another friend who is asleep, and goes on banging on the door of his house until he gets whatever he needs to provide the necessary meal.

It is only when we are genuinely concerned about the needs of those around us, and humbly realize our own spiritual emptiness, that we shall ask our heavenly Father for a fresh supply of the Spirit. If we are complacent, God has nothing to offer us. But if we are seriously seeking for God's Spirit to meet not only our needs but also the needs of others, then God will always fill the hungry with good things.

Jesus said, 'Happy are those whose greatest desire is to do what God requires; God will satisfy them fully!' (Matthew 5:6). Again he said, 'Whoever is thirsty should come to me and drink. . . . Whoever believes in me, streams of life-giving water [i.e. the Holy Spirit] will pour out from his heart' (John 7:37-38). God can renew us by his Spirit only when we are thirsty for him, longing to be the best for him. If that is true of you, Jesus promises that you will receive his Spirit in greater power if you ask him.

4. Unconfessed sin

The Spirit of God is the *Holy* Spirit. He will not fill a vessel that is unclean. We cannot make ourselves clean, but we can confess every known sin to God, repent of it, and then the blood of Jesus will cleanse us from all sin (1 John 1:7,9). Only after this can we be filled with the Holy Spirit.

Spend a few minutes quietly before God, asking his Spirit to search your heart to show you if there is anything that is not pleasing to God. What about your relationships? Your family life? Your work? Your use of time and money? What about your attitudes? What place has God in your life? Do you spend time praying to him? Do you try to serve him? Are you trying to help others to know and love him? Is there anything in your life about which your conscience is uneasy? Are you critical, touchy, resentful or bitter? Is there anyone whom you have not forgiven?

If we ask God to show us, we shall soon discover if there is anything in our life that we need to confess. Unless we are willing to do this, we cannot ask to be filled with the Holy Spirit.

5. Unbelief

Sometimes it is hard for us to believe that God will, or even can, do anything new in our lives. It may have happened in New Testament times. It may happen to others today. But somehow we do not think it will happen to us. We doubt if anything will be different.

Jesus knew all about the sin of unbelief in the human heart, so he prefaced the promise of the Spirit by saying: 'Ask, and you will receive; seek, and you will find; knock, and the door will be opened to you. For everyone who asks will receive, and he who seeks will find, and the door will be opened to anyone who knocks' (Luke 11:9-10). In effect he is saying: 'Do you find it hard to believe? Well, if you ask, it *will* happen, it *will* happen, it *will* happen....' He says it six times to make sure that we get the message!

It is important for us to grasp the nature of faith. Take, for example, the Christmas story. When the Virgin Mary was promised a gift of a son, she was puzzled. 'How can this be, since I have no husband?' The angel encouraged her faith by a series of promises: 'The Holy Spirit *will* come on you, and God's power *will* rest upon you...' (Luke 1:35). In other words, 'Mary, don't doubt! It *will* happen, it *will* happen!'

Mary then expressed her faith in two significant ways (Luke 1:38,46-49). First, there was the complete surrender of her life to the Lord: 'I am the Lord's servant; may it happen to me as you have said.' Second, she began to praise God that it was now already true!

My heart praises the Lord;
>my soul is glad because of God my Saviour,
>for he has remembered me, his lowly servant!
From now on all people will call me happy,
>because of the great things the Mighty God has done for me.

Here she praised God for what he *had* done for her, even though the actual experience and fulfilment of the promise was yet to come. But if God had promised it, as far as she was concerned it was already true!

That is the nature of true faith. Faith does not wait for experiences; faith does not depend on feelings. Faith takes God's word as it stands, believes it to be true, and starts praising God that it now *is* true, regardless of any feelings or experiences.

Many Christians wait for 'something' to happen before they will believe. God's order is the other way round. We must first believe the promise of God, and then something will happen — in God's own way and in God's own time. God deals with us all as individuals. Never make the mistake of looking for precisely the same experience of his Spirit that someone else may have had. It is the promise of God that counts. 'Whoever *believes* in me, streams of life-giving water will pour out from his heart' (John 7:38).

6. Fear

Fear is so common to us that the words 'Fear not' come in the Scriptures no less than 366 times — one for every day of the year, including leap year! Further, when God said 'Fear not', he was nearly always about to do something good and new in someone's life.

The devil loves to play on the cowardice of Christians! We are afraid of opening our hearts to God. We are afraid that we are not worthy of him. We wonder anxiously about what he may do in our lives. What changes will there be? What will he demand of me? What shall I be expected to do? Will I lose my reputation? Will I be making a fool of myself? Will I have to do things that I may not want to do? Will I have to stop doing things I may like doing now?

The answer to many of those questions is, frankly, yes! Jesus called the Holy Spirit the 'Comforter', but he may at times be a rather uncomfortable Comforter! The point is that God's plan for our lives is so much bigger and better than our own. He wants to redecorate the house of our life in a glorious way; but first we must be willing to throw out all the rubbish and to give him complete control. We must trust him that he knows what he is doing, and that he always works for our good. Never be afraid of letting God do what he wants with your life.

To show the foolishness of our fears Jesus said, 'Would any of you who are fathers give your son a snake when he asks for fish? Or would you give him a scorpion when he asks for an egg? Bad as you are, you know how to give good things to your children. How much more, then, will the Father in heaven give the Holy Spirit to those who ask him!' (Luke 11:11-13). There is no sting in the tail with God. He never plays tricks on his children.

How can you possibly lose if you open your life fully to the God who loves you more than you could ever possibly imagine, who understands everything about you, and who wants only the best for your life? He cares about you more than you could ever care about yourself. Indeed, you will find your full potential only when you are constantly filled with the Spirit of love, the Holy Spirit of God.

George T. Montague once put it beautifully like this: 'Can we say it more simply? Lovers have many ways of expressing their love, but especially two. One is by the words "I love you". The other is the kiss. God's word to me, reduced to essence, is "I love you". His Spirit, as the mystics long ago observed, is his kiss.' What does it mean, then, to be filled with the Spirit? 'It is simply allowing myself to be kissed.'

Don't be afraid of being 'kissed' by God, embraced by his love, filled with his Spirit.

Three things to remember

1. It is not once-for-all

When Paul wrote 'Be filled with the Spirit', the tense he used implied that we should go on being filled with the Spirit. It should be a continuous, daily, ever-fresh renewing. There may be a conscious first time — or there may not. What matters is the constant opening of our lives to the Spirit of God.

2. It is not the answer to all your problems

In fact it is the signal for some of the problems to begin! But they will be problems of life, not of death. When the Holy Spirit begins to work deeply in our lives, he may bring to the surface hidden wounds that need healing, long-standing attitudes that need correcting, some inner dross that needs purifying. Some of it may be painful, but always remember that God, in his infinite love, is seeking to change you into the likeness of Christ.

3. It is not just for personal blessing

It is to make you more effective as a Christian in God's church and in God's world. The Holy Spirit comes to guide you into God's perfect will for your life, and to fill your heart every day with the love of God — a love to be shared with others.

Time to act

If you have thought carefully through some of the hindrances, you need to obey the command to be filled with the Spirit and to claim Christ's promise that the Father will give the Spirit to those who ask him. If you are willing to let go anything you know is wrong in your life, and if you are prepared for Christ to be Lord of every part of your life, you can make this prayer your own.

First, be quiet and still in God's presence. Realize that he is with you and that he loves you. Now pray this prayer slowly and thoughtfully in your heart.

Heavenly Father, thank you that you love me and have given your Son for me.

I am sorry for every way in which I have hurt you, and grieved your Holy Spirit. I repent of everything in my life that I know is wrong. (Mention any specific sins on your conscience.)

I confess these sins to you, and humbly ask you to cleanse me from all sin.

I give myself afresh to you. I want Christ to be Lord of every part of my life: my personal life, my family life, my social life, my work, my time, my money, my relationships, my ambitions, my all. I want to love you with all my heart.

And now I ask you to fill me with your Holy Spirit.

Fill me with new life, new love, new joy, new strength.

Fill every part of my being, as humbly I claim the promise of your Son.

Fill me that I may live and work to your praise and glory.

Thank you, Father. I believe that you have heard my prayer.

I praise you and worship you.

Help me every day to go on being filled with your Spirit, that I may walk in your ways all the days of my life.

Through Jesus Christ our Lord. Amen.